MW01611565

A Day Spent With Mia 'n' Teddy

Story and illustrations by

Sandra A. McGuinness

A Day Spent With Mia 'n' Teddy

Story and illustrations by

Sandra A. McGuinness

PEAR
TREE
PUBLISHING

A Day Spent With Mia 'n' Teddy

Story & illustrations by Sandra A. McGuinness
Copyright © 2022 by Sandra A. McGuinness

Published by Pear Tree Publishing
Bradford, Massachusetts
www.PearTreePublishing.net

First Edition
Proudly published in the United States of America

McGuinness, Sandra, A.
 A Day Spent With Mia 'n' Teddy / by Sandra A. McGuinness — 1st Ed.

 ISBN 978-1-62502-049-9
 Library of Congress Control Number: 2021922289

 1. Children's – Author. 2. Children's – Lost & Found.
 3. Children's – Birthday 4. Children's – Adventure I. Title II. McGuinness, Sandra, A. III. Children's Book

Cover, Illustrations & Book Design by Sandra A. McGuinness

1,2,3,4,5,6,7,8,9,10

Dedication

To all parents and children to know how important it is to understand that discipline and love go hand in hand.

Mia was sound asleep one summer morning when Mom and Dad came into the room to wake her up. Mom said, "Mia, it's time for breakfast and we made your favorite pancakes!" Mia jumped out of bed and ran to the kitchen.

After Mia ate her pancakes Mom reminded her that today was her birthday. This was Mia's 6th birthday. Dad said, "We are going to a carnival!" Mia was so excited!

After breakfast, Mom and Dad gave Mia one of her birthday presents. Mia opened up the gift and pulled out a fluffy, adorable Teddy bear. A Teddy bear is something she had always wanted.

Mia loved Teddy's big red bow around his neck. The bow also had a tag on it that said, "To Mia, from Mom and Dad."

While Mom cleaned up the kitchen, Mia washed her face and hands and brushed her teeth. She then picked out her clothes and got dressed. Then Mom came in and brushed her hair.

Mia grabbed her headphones and Teddy and headed for the car. Mia put her seatbelt on and made sure to buckle up with Teddy on her lap.

Dad saw Mia with Teddy and suggested, "We'll leave Teddy at home so we won't lose him." Mia started to cry. Dad said, "Ok. Then we will just have to be careful not to lose him." Mia was so happy.

On the way to the carnival, Mia enjoyed listening to the music on her headphones. All of a sudden Mia heard loud music. She quickly took her headphone off one ear and looked out the window. She saw a big Ferris wheel, tents, lots of fun rides, and so many people. Mia yelled, "Wow!"

Dad parked the car and everyone got out. Dad noticed Mia holding Teddy. Dad and Mom told Mia she had to leave Teddy in the car. Mia was so upset and started to cry. Mia looked up at Mom and Dad and said, "I promise I will hold him tight and not lose him." Dad said, "Ok, we will watch Teddy too."

Mia chose her first ride which was the carousel. Mia held on to Teddy in her lap. Dad and Mom stayed on each side while the horse went up and down and all around. Mia had a smile from ear to ear.

After the carousel ride, Mom thought they should have something to eat. Mia wanted a hot dog. After they ate their hot dogs, Mia spotted an ice cream stand. Mia chose her ice cream flavor and asked for it in a sugar cone.

Mom, Dad, and Mia walked around as they ate their cones. They saw cotton candy stands, pinball machines, all kinds of games to win a prize, and funny looking clowns.

There were so many people and sure enough, somebody bumped into Mia and her ice cream fell to the ground. Mia was so sad but Dad went and got her another ice cream and had it put in a paper cup. Mom, Dad, and Mia went and sat on a bench and enjoyed the ice cream and all the excitement.

Mia spotted her next ride, the rollercoaster. Mia watched people laughing and yelling with excitement and throwing their arms up in the air. When they got to the rollercoaster, Dad got in first, then Mia and Teddy, and Mom last.

Mom, Dad, and Mia were laughing, arms up in the air, and then all of a sudden Teddy was flying through the air!

Dad saw the red bow and grabbed it. Dad said, "We were lucky." Mia held Teddy so tight and was so happy.

Dad noticed it was getting a little late in the day and said perhaps they could go on one more ride. Mia chose the Ferris wheel.

Dad got the tickets and then they had to wait for their seat to come down to the platform. They got in their seat, Teddy in the middle on Mia's lap. This ride was like being on top of the world!

Dad was showing Mia the ocean, the mountains, and all the people. They could also see all the different rides below.

Mia was yelling, "Happy Birthday to me!" She was laughing and waving to all the people. The ride lasted for quite a while but Mia wanted to go again!

Dad said, "No, it's getting late and it's time to head back home."

When Mom and Dad got off of the Ferris wheel, they realized someone was missing.

Mia screamed,

"Where is Teddy?"

Somehow, when pointing out all of the scenery, jumping up and down, laughing, and having a good time, Teddy must have fallen off Mia's lap.

Mia stayed with Mom while Dad went to search for Teddy. The attendant for the Ferris wheel was helping Dad too.

They looked everywhere and asked other people if they had seen a little brown Teddy bear with a big red bow. But they had no luck.

Mia was so sad with tears. They waited until all the riders had left their seats on the Ferris wheel. No one saw the Teddy bear. Dad decided to go to the Lost and Found area but had no luck there either.

Dad and Mom said, "Mia, we will get you a new Teddy bear, OK?" Mia said, "No, I want my Teddy bear."

As they were looking around the carnival, they heard a lady say to Mia, "Did you lose someone, little girl?" Mia said, "Yes." The lady said, "Was this someone a Teddy bear?" Mia said, "Yes." This nice lady held her hands behind her back hiding Teddy.

The nice lady asked one more question to make sure this Teddy was Mia's. The nice lady asked, "What was Teddy wearing?" Mia told her he was wearing a big red bow and a tag that said "To Mia, from Mom and Dad."

carnival

Then the nice lady took Mia's Teddy bear from behind her back. Mia was jumping up and down with happiness. Mom and Dad said, "What do you say to this nice lady?" Mia gave her a big hug and said, "Thank you, so much." Mia looked up at Mom and Dad and said, "I should have listened and left Teddy at home."

When Mia got home she was so surprised when she was greeted by Gramma and Grampa who came to visit for her birthday.

The kitchen table had a big birthday cake and balloons and presents for Mia.

After all the excitement, there was a happy ending to a day spent with Mia and Teddy!

For Parents and Teachers

This book is about how sometimes Mommies and Daddies make suggestions that may make you cry or unhappy. But Mommies and Daddies do this so you will learn to take care of things that are important to you.

But most of all, they do this because they love you and want you to be happy.

Acknowledgments

I would like to thank all of my family and friends for their support.

I would especially like to thank my publisher, Chris Obert. This past year had so many road blocks. With the pandemic and all of the delays that it caused, Chris kept me up on everything. This is my first book, and because of his help I had the confidence to go on. Chris is just the nicest person and by working together we made sure that my little book was published.

Made in the USA
Middletown, DE
06 April 2022

63485716R00020